Our HOME PLANET Earth

by Nancy Loewen   illustrated by Jeff Yesh

PICTURE WINDOW BOOKS
Minneapolis, Minnesota

Thanks to our advisers for their expertise, research, and advice:

Lynne Hillenbrand, Ph.D., Professor of Astronomy
California Institute of Technology

Terry Flaherty, Ph.D., Professor of English
Minnesota State University, Mankato

Editor: Jill Kalz
Designers: Amy Muehlenhardt and Angela Kilmer
Page Production: Melissa Kes
Art Director: Nathan Gassman
Associate Managing Editor: Christianne Jones
The illustrations in this book were created digitally.

Picture Window Books
5115 Excelsior Boulevard
Suite 232
Minneapolis, MN 55416
877-845-8392
www.picturewindowbooks.com

Printed in the United States of America.

All books published by Picture Window Books
are manufactured with paper containing at least
10 percent post-consumer waste.

Library of Congress Cataloging-in-Publication Data
Loewen, Nancy, 1964-
Our home planet : Earth / by Nancy Loewen ; illustrated by Jeff Yesh.
p. cm. — (Amazing science)
Includes index.
ISBN: 978-1-4048-3951-9 (library binding)
ISBN: 978-1-4048-3960-1 (paperback)
1. Earth—Juvenile literature. I. Yesh, Jeff, 1971 ill. II. Title.
QB631.4.L64 2008
525—dc22   2007032888

Table of Contents

What Do You See? 4

Discovering Earth 6

At Home in the Milky Way 8

Perfect for Life 10

A Blanket of Gases 12

Seasons, Days, and Years 14

A Changing Landscape 16

A Friend in Space 18

A Planet Called Home 20

Life on Earth 22

Fun Facts 23

Glossary 23

To Learn More 24

Index 24

What Do You See?

Look up at the night sky. Can you see the stars? How about the moon? Maybe you see the sparkling planet Venus. You might see the red glow of Mars or the pink glow of Jupiter.

Now imagine that you're in outer space, looking back at Earth. What does our planet look like?

Discovering Earth

In the last 50 years, we've put people on the moon. We've placed powerful telescopes in space. We're building a space station far above Earth's surface. We've sent spacecraft across millions of miles of our solar system to gather information.

We now know that our planet, Earth, looks like a beautiful marble from outer space. It glows a bright blue. White clouds swirl across it. Compared to the rest of our solar system, Earth is a small planet. And it is unusual in many ways.

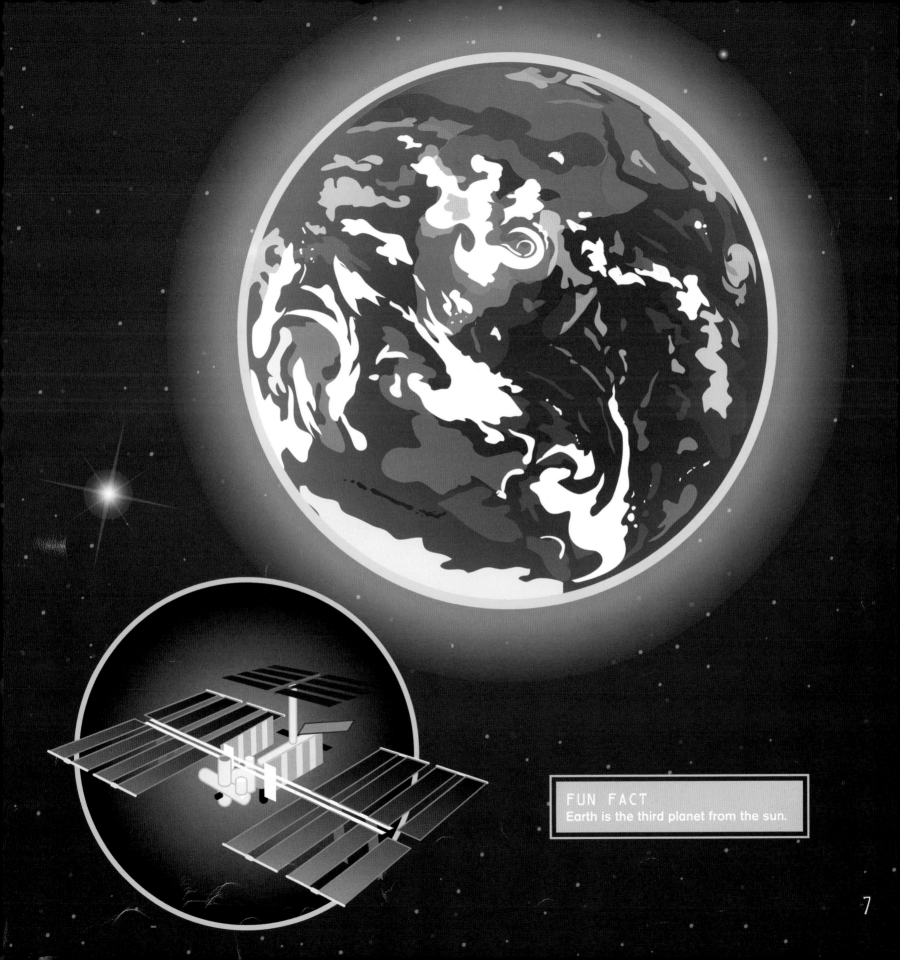

FUN FACT
Earth is the third planet from the sun.

At Home in the Milky Way

Like the seven other planets—Mercury, Venus, Mars, Jupiter, Saturn, Uranus, and Neptune—Earth circles around the sun. It is held in its orbit by the sun's gravity.

Tens of thousands of other objects circle around the sun, too. They include asteroids, dwarf planets, and comets. Together, these objects, the planets, and their moons make up our solar system.

The solar system, in turn, is part of a group of billions of stars called the Milky Way galaxy. Beyond the Milky Way lie billions of other galaxies.

Jupiter

Uranus

Neptune

Saturn

Mercury

Venus

Earth

Mars

FUN FACT
Not even the sun stays still in space. It circles,
or orbits, around the center of the galaxy,
taking the planets with it.

EDITOR'S NOTE
In this illustration, the distances between planets are not to
scale. In reality, the distances between the outer planets are
much greater than the distances between the inner planets.

Perfect for Life

Even among billions of galaxies, Earth is special. It is the only planet known to support life.

Water is needed for life, and Earth has a lot. More than 70 percent of the planet is covered by oceans.

The temperature on Earth also supports life. Earth is 93 million miles (149 million kilometers) away from the sun. If Earth were much closer to the sun, the planet would be too hot for life. If Earth were much farther away, it would be too cold.

FUN FACT
All of the water on Earth has been here for billions of years. It is constantly being recycled through the water cycle.

A Blanket of Gases

Earth's blanket of gases, or atmosphere, helps support life, too.
These gases trap heat from the sun and keep Earth from getting too
cold. At the same time, they block many harmful rays from the sun.

Earth's atmosphere is made of 78 percent nitrogen and 21 percent oxygen. There are also small amounts of argon, carbon dioxide, and water vapor.

FUN FACT
Earth's atmosphere is special among the planets. It has the most oxygen.

Seasons, Days, and Years

Earth is tilted and turns on its center, or axis. The four seasons—spring, summer, fall, and winter—happen because of this tilt. As Earth orbits the sun, some areas of the planet receive more light than others. When an area on Earth is tilted toward the sun, it has summer. When an area is tilted away from the sun, it has winter. Summer in Earth's northern hemisphere is winter in Earth's southern hemisphere.

FUN FACT
Earth takes about 24 hours to turn, or rotate, on its axis. One complete rotation equals one day. It takes 365 days for Earth to orbit around the sun. One complete orbit equals one year.

A Changing Landscape

Earth's outer layer, or crust, is made of large sections called plates. These plates are always moving. Over millions of years, they might push into each other and form mountains. They also might pull away. Sometimes the plates grind past each other and cause earthquakes.

Volcanoes release molten rock from deep within the planet. This rock changes Earth's surface both on land and beneath the oceans. Wind and water also wear down the landscape. They move bits of rock and soil from place to place.

FUN FACT
Earth is divided into four main layers: a thin crust, a thick mantle made of rock, an outer core made mostly of molten iron and nickel, and an inner core made mostly of solid iron and nickel.

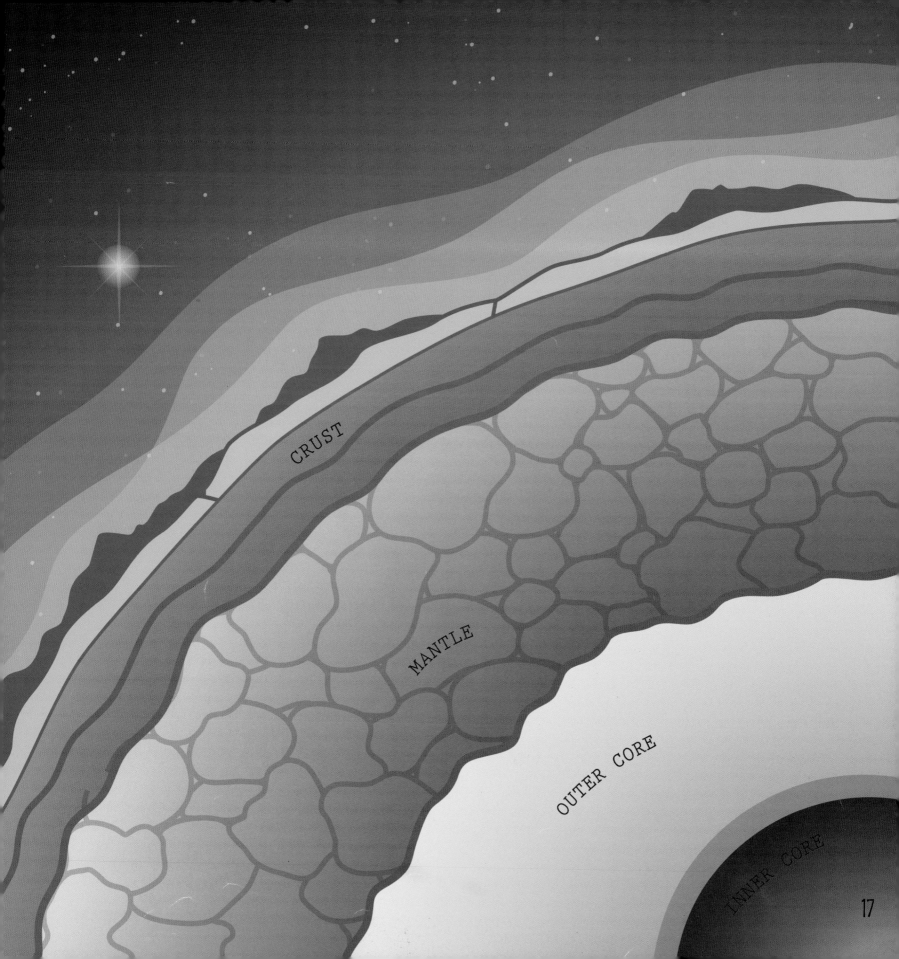

CRUST

MANTLE

OUTER CORE

INNER CORE

17

A Friend in Space

As Earth orbits the sun, the moon orbits Earth. The moon is much smaller than Earth. Its diameter is about one-fourth of Earth's diameter.

Earth's moon may have once been a part of Earth itself. More than 4 billion years ago, a small planet may have crashed into Earth and knocked part of it off. The rocks and dust came together to form the moon.

Earth's gravity then captured the moon and kept it in orbit ever since. But the moon's gravity affects Earth, too. The moon's gravity creates tides, the daily rising and falling of the ocean.

FUN FACT
Earth has one moon. Mercury has no moons.
Jupiter and Saturn have at least 55 moons each!

A Planet Called Home

Earlier, you imagined what Earth would look like from far away. You thought about its place in our solar system and in our galaxy.

Now, take a look around you. How many kinds of life do you see? Maybe you see trees, flowers, and grass. Maybe you see your dog wagging its tail, or an ant crawling along the ground, or a good friend waving hello.

We live on a pretty terrific planet, wouldn't you say?

Life on Earth

What you need:

- old magazines
- scissors
- a piece of paper, any color
- a glue stick
- a bowl or large can
- a pencil
- a larger piece of paper, blue or black

What you do:

1. Look through the magazines and tear out pictures that have to do with life on Earth. Include pictures of the sky, the ocean, landscapes, plants, animals, and people. Try to get a lot of different colors.

2. Now, cut out smaller pieces of the pictures you chose. You can make them whatever shapes you'd like.

3. Glue your pictures onto the piece of paper. You can overlap them or arrange them in patterns.

4. Turn your paper over. Using the bowl or large can, trace a circle.

5. Cut out your circle and glue it onto the blue or black paper. Now you have a beautiful mini Earth!

Fun Facts

- If Earth's orbit were a perfect circle, it would always be the same distance from the sun. But its orbit is shaped like an oval, so at times Earth is closer and at times it's farther from the sun. That's why we say Earth is an "average" distance of 93 million miles (149 million km) from the sun.

- Earth is the fifth-largest planet in the solar system. Its diameter is 7,926 miles (12,682 km). The planet isn't perfectly round. It bulges a bit at the equator.

- A solar eclipse happens when the moon passes directly between Earth and the sun, blocking the sun's light. A lunar eclipse happens when Earth passes directly between the moon and the sun.

Glossary

asteroid—a rock that circles around the sun

atmosphere—the gases that surround a planet

comet—an icy ball that orbits the sun

diameter—the distance of a line running from one side of a circle, through the center, and across to the other side

dwarf planet—a planet-like body that has not yet made a clear orbit for itself

galaxy—a large group of billions of stars, planets, and other matter such as dust and gas

gravity—the force that pulls things down toward the surface of a planet

hemisphere—one half of Earth

orbit—the path an object takes to travel around a star or planet; also, to travel around a star or planet

solar system—the sun and the bodies that orbit around it; these bodies include planets, moons, dwarf planets, asteroids, and comets

telescope—a device with mirrors or lenses; a telescope makes faraway objects appear closer

To Learn More

More Books to Read

Hall, Cally, and Scarlett O'Hara. *1001 Facts About Planet Earth.* New York: DK Pub., 2003.

Rau, Dana Meachen. *Earth.* Minneapolis: Compass Point Books, 2003.

Simon, Seymour. *Earth: Our Planet in Space.* New York: Simon & Schuster Books for Young Readers, 2003.

On the Web

FactHound offers a safe, fun way to find Web sites related to topics in this book. All of the sites on FactHound have been researched by our staff.

1. Visit *www.facthound.com*
2. Type in this special code: 1404839518
3. Click on the FETCH IT button.

Your trusty FactHound will fetch the best sites for you!

Index

atmosphere, 12, 13
color, 4, 6
galaxy, 8, 9, 10, 20
layers, 16
location, 7, 11, 23
moon, 4, 6, 18, 19, 23
orbit, 8, 9, 14, 15, 18, 19, 23
seasons, 14
size, 6, 23
temperature, 11, 12
water, 10, 11, 16

Look for all of the books in the Amazing Science: Planets series:

Brightest in the Sky: The Planet Venus
Dwarf Planets: Pluto, Charon, Ceres, and Eris
Farthest from the Sun: The Planet Neptune
The Largest Planet: Jupiter
Nearest to the Sun: The Planet Mercury
Our Home Planet: Earth
Ringed Giant: The Planet Saturn
Seeing Red: The Planet Mars
The Sideways Planet: Uranus